P9-CQD-948

wrinkles

To our grandparents
– JR & JP

A SPECIAL THANKS TO:
Emile Abinal, Marc Azoulay, Marco Berrebi, Quentin Besnard,
Melvyn Bonnaffé, Mauve Chalandon, Marion Charlot, Valentin Crepain,
Selin Delamare, Lucca Fletcher, Julie Haudry-Hurault, Maud Malfettes,
Camille Pajot, Luana Saltiel, Jaime Scatena, Lisa Truchassout,
Prune, Loïc, Etan, Noémie, Maryse, Gérard, and Elsa

wrinkles

by JR

We all have eyes,
We all have a nose,
We all have a mouth . . .

. . . And some of us have wrinkles.

They appear as we get older,

Like soft stripes

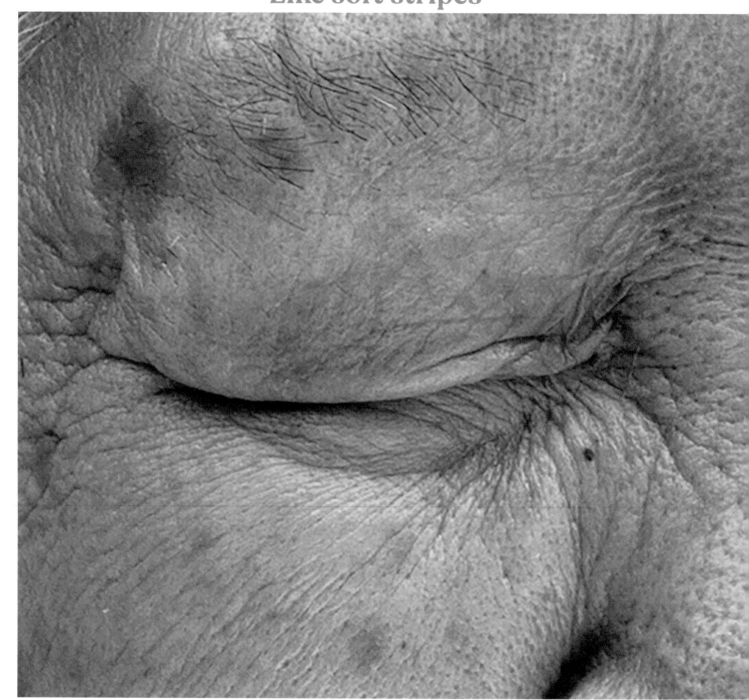

in our skin.

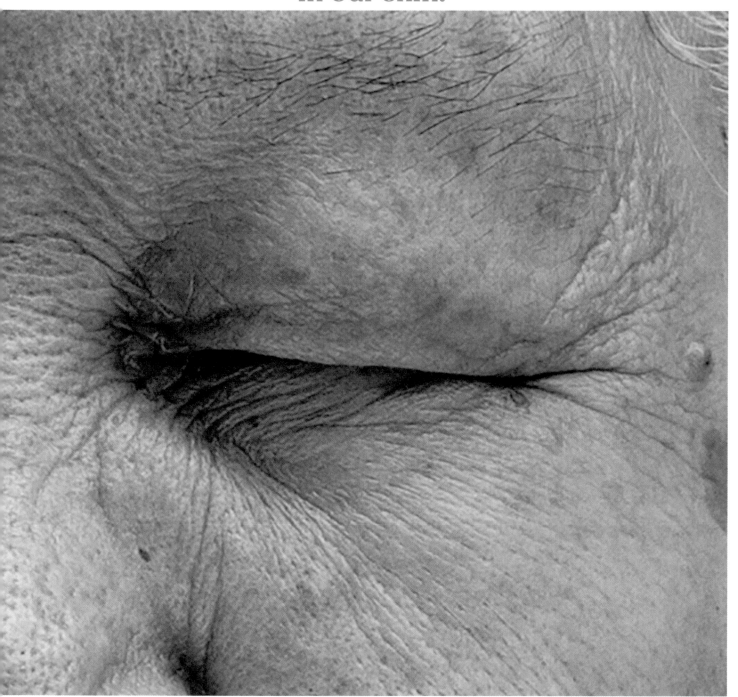

The older you are,

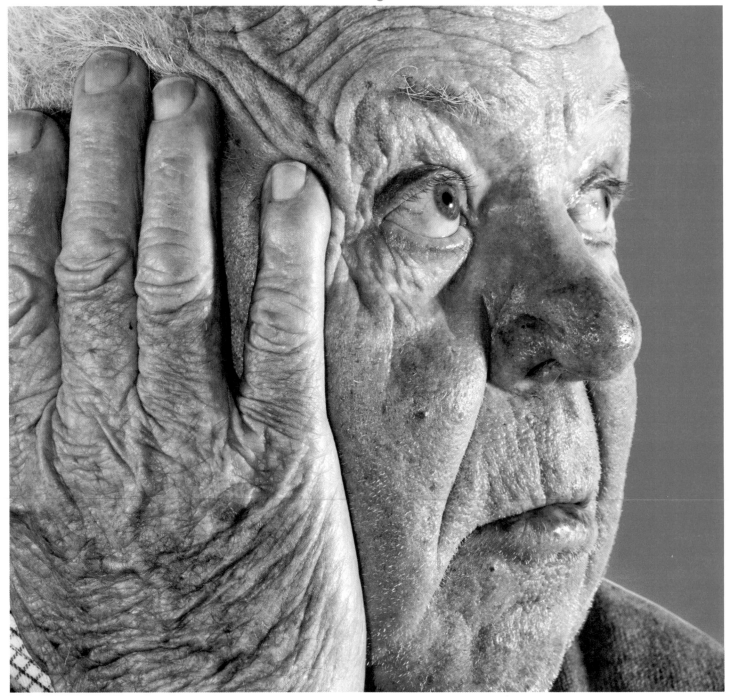

the more wrinkles you wear!

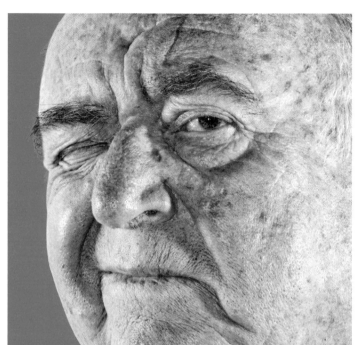

Wrinkles tell the story

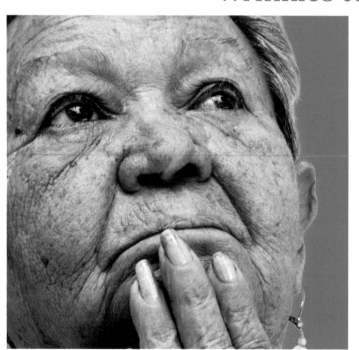

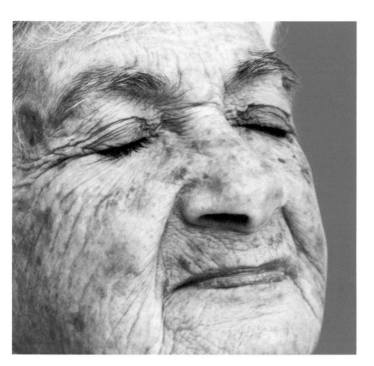

of someone's life:

Of laughter,

And togetherness;

Of play,

And calm;

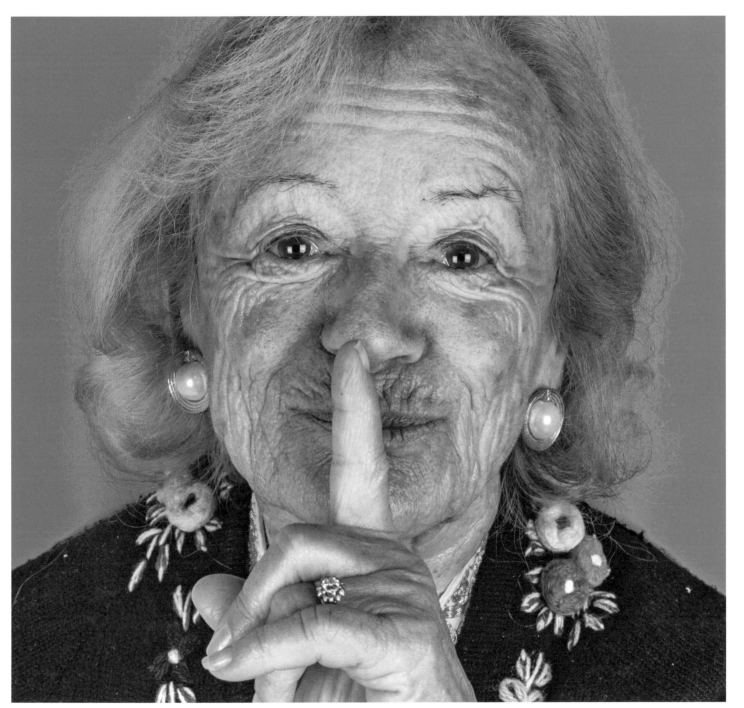

Of secrets

And wisdom.

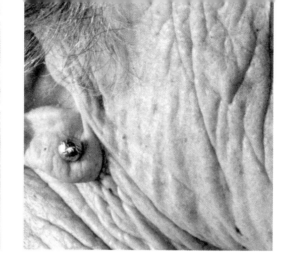

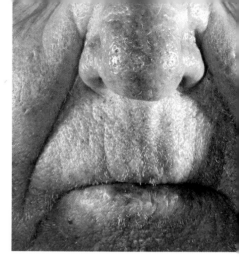

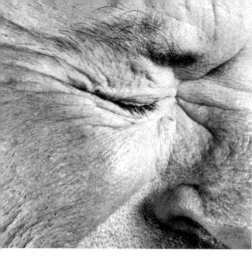

These stories
surround you

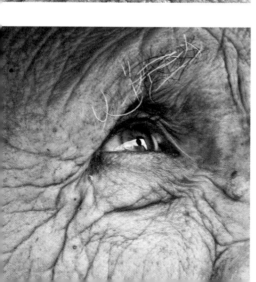

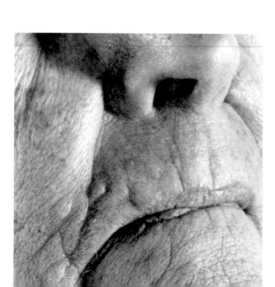

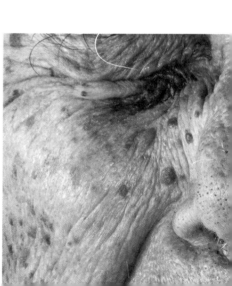

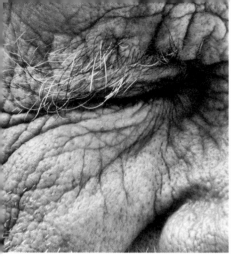
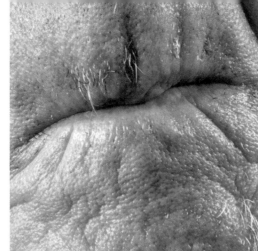
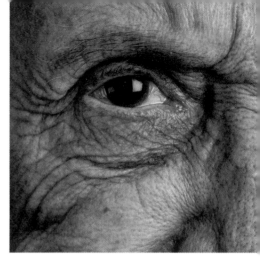

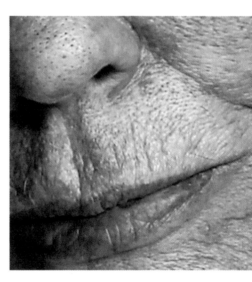

In the wrinkles
all around you.

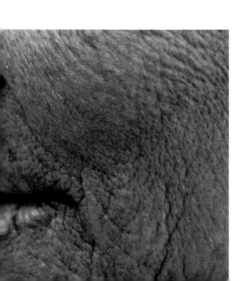
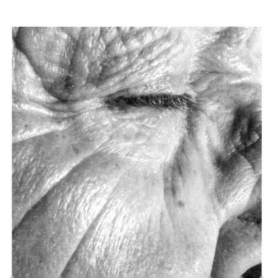
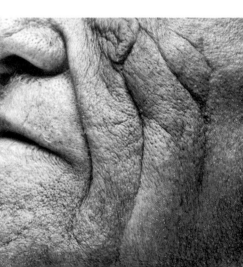

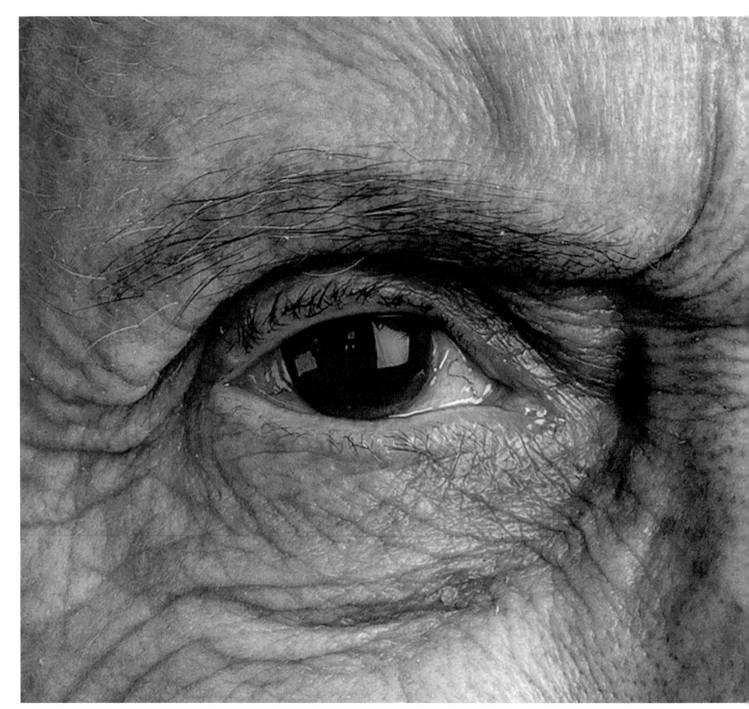

Whose wrinkles do you see?

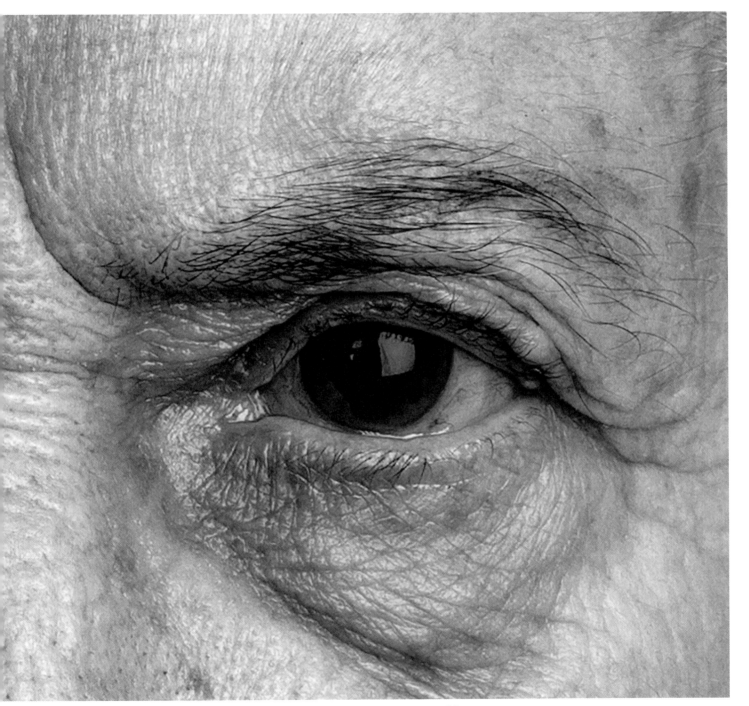

What can they tell you?

The Stories Behind the Wrinkles in This Book

My name is Antonio Sanchez Sorroche. I am 82 and I live in Cartagena, Spain. When I was young, my sister and I went from bar to bar, playing the guitar and the bandurria (a Spanish stringed instrument, similar to a mandolin) to earn money. We were paid just a few coins for our music. Later I became the manager of a bar.

My name is Jin Kaiyue. I am 86 and I was born in Shanghai, China. I have two daughters. One of them is 50 years old and lives on the same street as me. She is a doctor. I retired 20 years ago. I used to work on boats as an engineer, repairing machines.

My name is Rolando Victor Jimenez Briganti. I am 91 but I was only 14 when I moved to Havana, Cuba. I worked in a few shops first, then in a hotel. After that, I worked in a metal factory, and then I was a truck driver for 10 years. Now I sell sweets and cigarettes.

My name is José Martinez Roca and I am 84. I grew up in Cartagena, Spain and met my wife here as well. We have five children: three boys and two girls. Cartagena has changed a lot. When I was a child, it was all fields. Now there are buildings and factories everywhere.

My name is Ada Claudina Pupo Mastrapa. I live in old Havana – a special, historical part of Havana city in Cuba. My father worked very hard and my mother was a great mother. I got married young, at 15, and I devoted my life to my three children. I have had a good life.

My name is Tuangpet Kunavantanit. I was born in Thailand, but my sister convinced me to move to America. Everything is wonderful here. I went back to Thailand to take care of my family for a few years, but then I moved back to America. Now I live with my sister in Los Angeles.

My name is Luisa Maria Miranda Oliva. I am 88 and I was born in the province of Matanzas in Cuba. I first got married when I was 18 and I came to live in Havana. I lost my first husband after 21 years of marriage, but I got married a second time. I have always been a country girl: I really liked swimming in rivers and I love nature.

My name is Nidia Mulet Rojas and I am 75. I was born in Holguin in Cuba. We were a family of eight brothers and sisters, and we lived happily. I moved to Havana because of health problems. I fell in love, got married, and have lived here for the past 50 years. I really like going to museums, as well as looking at mural paintings.

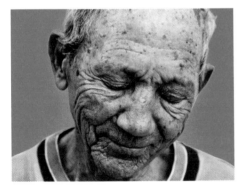

My name is Alfonso Ramon Fontaine Batista. I am 83, and I am from the Eastern part of Cuba. I live in Havana now, but I prefer living in the country to living in the city. I do all sorts of jobs. I am a woodworker and a builder, I am also a baker and a butcher. I love all these jobs.

My name is Barbara Kaplan and I am 93. I left New York for Los Angeles because it was too cold. My husband and I drove all the way from New York to California in a truck. I used to work with old people. I created a multiservice space for them; it was a fabulous experience.

My name is Shi Li and I live in Shanghai, China. I have six children who were all government employees. They are now retired. I even have a great-grandchild. They all love me and that makes me very happy.

My name is Helga Nippa. I am 79 and I live in Berlin, Germany. I used to be a nurse. My husband and I met at nursing school. We have now been married for 60 years. We have also worked as actors in several films together. They were so much fun.

My name is Rafael Lorenzo. I was born a musician. I have been to many cities, thanks to music. My wife, Obdulia Manzano, and I have lived in Havana, Cuba for 40 years. We got married 60 years ago. My wife has never left Havana because she loves her home and never wants to leave it.

My name is Julio Batista. I am 70 and I was born in Havana, Cuba. I have been working at a cranes and towing unit of a maritime service company for 59 years. I have also worked at a laundrette.

My name is Milagros Vallejo Herrero. I live in Cartagena, Spain, and I am 88. I was a baker's daughter, and one of nine children. Everyone worked for the family business. I was in charge of selling bread in the closest villages. I used to ride our horse to get to the villages. I would ride at the fastest speed.

My name is Frederico Sanchez and I am 76. I'm from Cartagena, Spain, where I have lots of friends. I love sports and have enjoyed many sports in my lifetime, especially judo, football, and walking. I have seven children. My wife died from cancer.

My name is Onelia Lopez Ruiz and I was born in Santiago de Cuba, where there is a fantastic carnival. Later, I moved to Havana. I have four children. We've had some difficult times in Cuba but we all live in peace now. I am a little old lady and a happy grandmother.

My name is Okay Temiz and I am 76 and I live in Istanbul, Turkey. As a child, I lived on a farm with tractors and animals around me. When I grew up, everything became about jazz music. I am a percussionist. I have played music all over the world.

My name is Lili Barokas and I live in Istanbul. I've always loved music and dance. I was a ballet teacher and I have been teaching ballet for as long as I can remember. I believe all children should learn ballet. I also used to travel every year to all kinds of places: America, Asia, Australia, North of Africa…and more. I loved it!

My name is Maria Corbalan Fernandez and I am 88. I was born in Cartagena, Spain. I did not go to school as I needed to help my family. I started working as a house servant when I was 11. When I got married, my husband and I moved to the La Palma area in Spain, and we worked in the fields to earn a living.

My name is Mariano Saura Oton. I am 73 and I was born in Cartagena, Spain. When I was 15, I started to work for an international shipping company. I worked at the same company until my retirement. I love the harbor in Cartagena. It's Cartagena's treasure.

My name is Encarnacion Garcia Martinez. I am 80 and I live in Cartagena. I was the youngest of 14 children. When I was 11, I started taking care of animals and collecting firewood to help my big family. When I grew up and had my own three children, I stopped working outside and we decided to move to another village.

My name is Miguel Pelegrino. I'm 88 years old and I live in Havana, Cuba. I used to work for the State. I had a job at a hospital. Now I sell shopping bags.

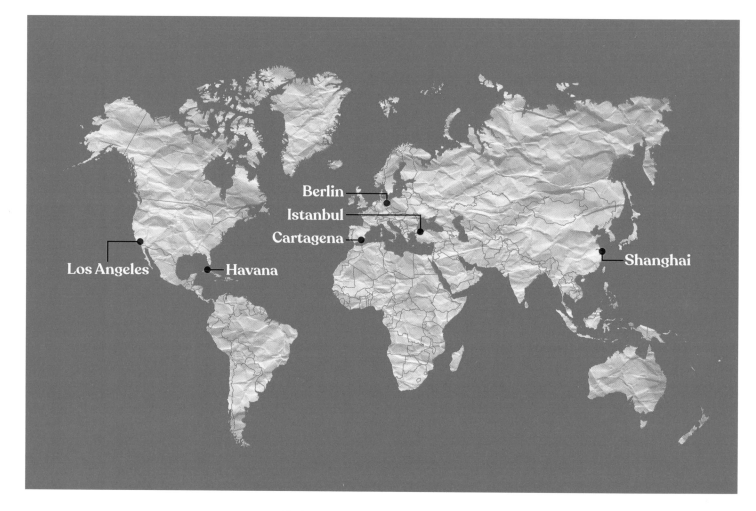

Berlin
Istanbul
Cartagena
Los Angeles
Havana
Shanghai

Wrinkles Around the World

The photos in this book were part of a project by the artist JR called The Wrinkles of the City. It took place in six cities across the world, starting in Cartagena in Spain, and continued in Shanghai, China; Havana, Cuba (in collaboration with the artist José Parlà); Los Angeles, USA; Berlin, Germany; and Istanbul, Turkey. Each of these cities has changed a lot during the last 100 years. JR wanted to record these changes through portraits of the oldest members of each city.

He took photos, recorded the stories of these people, and pasted large black-and-white pictures of them across the buildings and walls of each city. Every person had unique stories and memories to share. Many had lived, worked, and grown families in these cities. When some of them were children, their cities barely had any buildings. Some lived through war. These giant portraits represent the stories of people who have witnessed each city's changing history firsthand.

About JR

I am an artist. I take portraits of people all around the world. I print these portraits of women and men onto huge sheets of paper in black-and-white. Then I paste them onto the walls of cities across the world with paper and glue. I paste them onto houses, large buildings, and even on streets, so that everyone can see them. For me, cities are like giant art galleries: even those who don't usually visit museums get to see my work. Exhibiting these photographs in cities is also a way for people who might be unknown in a city to be seen by everyone. It's a way to get people wondering about who these men and women are, and for them to share their stories — their memories, their experiences, their lives. These stories get people thinking and talking, and can change the way people see each other and the way we see the world. A lot of people and communities participate in my projects, perhaps one day you can, too!

Pic
J
JR
Main

YOUTH SERVICES
Falmouth Public Library
300 Main Street
Falmouth, MA 02540
508-457-2555

Phaidon Press Limited
Regent's Wharf
All Saints Street
London N1 9PA

Phaidon Press Inc.
65 Bleecker Street
New York, NY 10012

phaidon.com

First published 2019
Copyright © 2019 Phaidon Press Limited
Text © Julie Pugeat
Projects and artworks © JR

About JR section: photos by Marc Azoulay, Fabien Barrau

Typeset in Recoleta Semibold
and Circular Pro Book

ISBN 978 1 83866 016 1
004-0719

A CIP catalogue record for this book is available from the
British Library and the Library of Congress. All rights reserved.
No part of this publication may be reproduced, stored in a
retrieval system or transmitted, in any form or by any means,
electronic, mechanical, photocopying, recording or otherwise,
without the written permission of Phaidon Press Limited.

Designed by Meagan Bennett
Printed in China